kaleidoscope

of colors

Robert A. Cozzi

For information, address Beach Umbrella Publishing 1834 SE 5th
Street, Cape Coral, Florida 33990

LIBRARY OF CONGRESS CATALOGING IN
PUBLICATION DATA

Cozzi, Robert A.

       kaleidoscope of colors /by Robert A. Cozzi

ISBN- 978-0-578-44190-0

ISBN-10: 0-578-44190-X

First Edition: January 2019

FOREWORD

"The kaleidoscope symbolizes the release of blocked creativity and it gives you the opportunity to see yourself in the bigger scope of life, and connect to the meaning of it. The various colors and forms in a kaleidoscope can symbolize your escape in time of difficulty and self-doubt."

Robert asked me to write the foreword to his 5th book of poetry and prose. It's difficult for a plethora of reasons to put into words my relationship with the poet. I came into contact with Robert I would like to say right around 10 years ago, when YouTube was just starting up and not many people realized what that social media site was capable of; before ads were even on YouTube, to just give the reader a feeling of how long ago this was. Robert would give me words of encouragement on my melody and I would read his words of stanza and rhyme. In a short synopsis of myself I am a self-proclaimed singer songwriter who by self-imposed muscle memory played in shadows and alleyways that snuffed out my flame for a long while and just until recently I found that light again. I know what it is to be cold and lost, hungry and alone. I longed to play the blues and now I have lived them, I have escaped times of difficulty and self-doubt and by the fates would have it; maybe Robert is more of a genius I give him credit for, I am the perfect medium to write this foreword. Kudos, Robert, raise of the glass to you sir.

When you start reading "kaleidoscope of colors" the first few poems that stuck out to me were "My Utopia" The proverbial mirage of the creature comfort you long for, we all long for. The last line," 'This is my dream." So finite. Cold and warm at the same time. The poem 'Cast Off," a writing style Robert has not tapped into, he flirts with the alleyways I once called home. A cynicism I have not read in Robert's words up until this point. The poem "Damn" A sensual snake slithering up bed posts as deep delta blues fill the room with a red glow of sex and sweaty anticipation and then, at the blink of an eye, gone, the mirage again. Just at the tip of our fingers, the tips of our tongues. Just one little taste and I'll be good! I promise, but that sweet sodden taste never submits. Longing only an ex-heroin addict can relate to or an individual who's heart demands to envelope itself with fairy-tale love and never gets their "happily ever after."

Robert has stayed in touch with me throughout these years; years in which I lost touch with the closest of friends and family and to be honest reality itself at times. Periodically messaging me like the tenacious and caring east coast jiminy cricket that he is and making sure I'm still above ground. It's a strange feeling of knowing true authenticity. That's the best compliment I can give someone in my opinion, being authentic. In this narcissistic, plastic, choose which filter is perfect world, Robert Cozzi has been nothing but real and at times the smelling salt I needed when I was lost. Robert you have done things for me I will not mention in detail but you know I will forever call you a friend and always be there in your time of need, if and whenever that may come.

Reading this book has been an ever changing trail of ups, downs, cold and warm rhythmic meters. Almost manic at times. Words have not captivated me and kept my attention since Bukowski. "The Explorer," had me at a loss for words. The acceptance of darkness, the vantablack chasm, reminding me of the story of the Russian cosmonaut who has been trapped in the abyss with a "ticking sound" that escapes him and inevitably drives him mad until he learns to love and accept the sound of this soft ticking. "Gentleness of touch, Blades placed away." Brilliant, Robert. In my humble opinion this is the best writing you have done; you have tapped into a well that has unleashed what you can provide to the world and to art itself. The word "art" has lost its allure; the gold-bearing veins have been sucked dry by charlatans and redundant conveyor belt "poets." And you my friend are a rare deposit that's been hiding on a quiet meadow mountain side waiting to be found when you are ready, and again in my humble opinion I believe this book will be your "gold rush."

I will end this forward with a brief thought on your last poem in the book, "To the young Artists." The first line, "Enhance this world." This says it all. Nothing you have shown me in our 10+ years has expressed anything else but a selfless individual who genuinely wants to paint the void with his passion of words and pull others from the plastic purple estates, inspire and show what literature can do for not himself but the world around him and others. To step into the darkness with a steady hand, to be a soldier of beauty, love and art and show what it means to imprint a melody, a stanza, a softly painted picture in one's heart, mind and soul. You are a rare gem my friend. I thank you for this opportunity and with a full heart I say this is your best work. Flip through these pages reader, take time to let the words manifest different lights, shapes, and sounds from your own experiences of love, longing, heartbreak and healing. Allow these kaleidoscopes of colors to paint your own intimate picture.

- Cody James

Dedication:

I would like to dedicate this book of work:

To my late friend, Jerome Gonzalez, you will forever remain deep inside my heart and your spirit continues to inspire the words I write.

To my Mom and Dad, I miss you every day.

To Annmarie, Michael, Nicholas, Nick, Danni, and Kai with love.

To my Bard Brother, Chayce, you make me a better writer.

Acknowledgements:

I would like to express my thanks to:

Gerard Yatcilla, Mary Healy Davis, Ian Tompkins, Trish Bizink Abell, Donna Catanzaro, Michelle Osterberg, Lisa Hafler, Larry Osterberg, Jo Ann Carra, Jim Kurzawa, Anthony Rivera, Bryan Glenn, Jamie Treglown, Matthew Ryan Woolfrey, Anne Laird, Paul Kocum, Tai Babilonia, Loretta Obstfeld, Ed Burgos, Gabby Parraga, Phillip Piedad, Cody Conner, Carlin Rose, Don Jeanes, Adrian Collazo, Noelle Deniger, Megan Smith, J.J. Shah, Charles

Ryan Smith, Nathaniel Chin, Jaime Rivera, Michael Galante, Jon Foreman, Annemarie Biondi, Glenn Randall, Davian Williams, Jamie Lamarra, Lynn Sadler, Jaime Schneider, Mary King Treglown, Jorge Alarcon, Shaun Daley, Michelle Pankowski Kassick, Phillip Wilcher, Sandy Iammatteo, Walt Clarkson, Kristin Nascelli, Mr. and Mrs. Randhawa, Stevie Nicks, The Town Book Store, my Saturday morning story hour kids from the library, and my Facebook and Instagram followers and friends.

AUTHOR'S NOTE

Why must we always feel the need to explain emotions …
even good ones? If one is smiling then someone will
undoubtedly ask, "What are you so happy about?" And
likewise if you shed tears then someone will ask, "What is
wrong?" It is like the norm is to have that dead pan straight
line look of utter boredom and apathy to be left alone. You
have to maintain a subway passenger face.

Emotions are tricky devils aren't they? They mess you up.
They interfere with normal day to day activities. They cloud
your reason. They delude your thinking. I have always been
full of exaggerated and sometimes deep emotion. Everything
is urgent, powerful, and dramatic! I wonder if that is the price
to pay for having a creative and imaginative mind that never
stops. Either way, I wouldn't change a thing. I like these parts
of me.

The dark side of emotions can be difficult, but as Stevie
Nicks says, "You have to survive the nightmare to get to the
dream." And I think she would know.

It is part of life to suffer. Everyone does it. Pain is the great
equalizer for us all. People feel it in different ways … express
it in even more of a variety of ways. There is no right way to
do it although some will tell you differently.

Sometimes pain is a wake-up call. Sometimes it sets about
change that otherwise wouldn't happen. Sometimes the pain
tells us to listen, to be quiet, and to find ourselves again in the
stillness. And sometimes pain is to be shared with a fellow
traveler on a crossed path, which is one of the reasons I write.

It is all a part of the human experience.

Thank you for purchasing my book, "kaleidoscope of colors." I hope you enjoy reading my words.

Robert A. Cozzi

__KALEIDOSCOPE COLORS__

His desires

Of kaleidoscope colors

Rise to meet

The rainbow of common truth

JUMPING OFF THE SHELF

The steps in front of you

Used to lead right back

To the same old promises

You kept on the shelf

But this journey launches a new beginning

Unlike the missteps before

Because this time

Each step leads to

An open door

MY UTOPIA

Searching out

Trying to find another to fill a void

And then

When found

We shower each other with

Love

And once deep commitments are made

It allows two people

To move as one

Merging

Until

If one bleeds

The other soul hurts too

This is my dream

THE STREET ARTIST

The spray paint spills

Crimson and cobalt onto the wall

Complexities shown in demanding lines, angles, and zigzags

Begging to capture

Someone's eye

TWIN FLAMES

The complexity

And simplicity of our frequency

Is astounding

Measuring heartbeats in minutes

Within a moment

We are two in separate lives

Living out separate moments

But still we roam

Back to one another

DROWNING IN WORDS

When the words come

Everything else

Disappears

The suffocating room

Fills with air

And intense emotions

Overflow

Flooding everything

Until I am drowning

In words

18

THE WALK

The late September sunlight

Swims into our daydreams

As we walk together

On a quiet path

Covered with

The first fallen

Red and orange leaves of autumn

Branches crackle beneath our feet

Our destination is unknown

Silence ensues

And no words are spoken

Occasionally

We catch each other's eye

And smile

I love how we don't even have to talk

To enjoy each other's company

We both chuckle

When our silence is interrupted

By the high school marching band playing up ahead

Their musical echo fills the neighborhood

And keeps us company

As we make the turn for home

PRIVATE PERFORMANCE

My spirits lift

When I hear the intro

And imagine the artist

Raising their instrument

And playing

      Just for me ...

MYSTERY

The table lies as it was left this morning

Oatmeal becoming stale in its white bowl

The spoons fogged with the residue of food and breath

The chairs pushed haphazardly out at angles

The green sneakers still lie by the door

Laces untied and one tipped to the left side

As if someone was just about to pull them on

The pages of a book flutter in the stale air

Until even the back cover flops over with a thud

Losing the place of the person whom was surely

About to return and softly flip its pages

Where is the life that once held this place in its lively and determined grip?

ROBERT AND JEROME

Our friendship

Was the most beautiful surprise

Because in the beginning

We were anything but friends

But as the time passed

We began to understand one another more

And an artistic bond was born

The kind that is so hard to find

Now that the days we had are gone

I live in silence every morning

Since you died

Because my days always began

With our morning conversations

24

Turning slowly

And looking down at my paper

There are no words

I can write

That can save me

Because I am broken

And I'm pissed …

No more laughing with you

No more pictures or drawings of yours to see

No more deep conversations

No more mutual inspiration

But if you were here now

You would tell me,

"Open your eyes, Robert and let go of the anger.

Be the man I once knew.

And keep writing, creating and loving."

So here I am

Writing …

Living the life of an artist

The very lifestyle that saved us both

I miss you every day

And hope that one day

We can meet again …

CAST OFF

The cellophane personality

Of a disloyal lover

Puts his thoughts

In disarray

But with precise

Dictation

Their words are spoken

Declaring each their stance

Leaving his illusion

Of love

Broken

And his heart

Cast off

As bait

In shark infested waters

SCREAMING HEART

I wonder if you can feel

The heart that screams out your name

In the middle of the night

From the outside edge

Of your dreams …

JULIAN

It was April of 2011, and I was a graduate student at NYU working my Master's Degree. I had settled into my daily routine of beginning my day at work at the hotel before making the trek to the city for afternoon and evening classes. I was a pretty unlikely, "New Yorker," but I'd managed to acclimate myself nonetheless.

My last class that day finished at 9:45pm and I took the Path over to Newark Penn Station as usual, but they were experiencing signal problems that night so my train home was delayed indefinitely. Sitting in the station, I took out my class notes and began rewriting them, figuring I should make the most of my time. I was hungry too and glad that I had saved the other half of my ham and cheese sandwich for the train ride home.

As a rule, I try to avoid eye contact when I am in Newark Penn Station, so I was more than a little unsettled when I felt a pair of eyes staring in my direction. I remembered noticing a young soldier dressed in army fatigues sitting on the bench across from me as I entered the waiting room earlier, so when I finally looked up I wasn't all that surprised that he was the one staring, but he was not looking at me, he was looking at my sandwich. When we did make eye contact he was embarrassed and looked away. I asked him if he was hungry and he said, "yes,' while avoiding my eyes. I walked over and sat next to him. He could not have been more than 20 or 21 years old. I introduced myself while extending my hand to shake his. He had a strong grip and told me that his name was Julian and that he had just finished a tour in Iraq. As we spoke more, he became a bit more comfortable and even looked me in the eye and gave me a small smile when I thanked him for his service. So when I suggested that we head over to the 24 hour McDonald's to get him something to eat, he agreed and ordered a double quarter pounder meal with fries and a vanilla shake. We settled down at one of the tables near the train departures board. Julian explained that he had come home to New Jersey to live with his cousin and her family, but that situation turned out to be temporary. And now he desperately needed to find work and a place to stay. He told me that his grandmother had raised him, but she died shortly after he enlisted. The desperation in his eyes broke my heart, and I knew that I wanted to help him get back on his feet.

I knew a hotel colleague who was the night manager at one the airport hotels in Newark, so I called and asked if he needed any van drivers, valet parking attendants, or security officers. As it turned out, he was looking for a van driver. I quickly told him about Julian and asked if he had some time now to speak with the young soldier. Julian had already wolfed down his food and was excited to show me his driver's license and said that he would jump at the chance to be a driver at the hotel.

Making our way over to the cab stand, we said our goodbyes. Julian insisted on getting my address because he wanted to pay me back for the food and the cab. I told him that it wasn't necessary, but I wanted to stay in touch, so I gave him my work address and phone number. As the cab pulled away, I called my hotel friend back to say that Julian was on his way and asked him to please call me later to let me know how everything turned out.

I didn't hear anything until the next morning when my hotel friend called to tell me that he had hired Julian and had given him a temporary place to stay. A few weeks later, I received a money order in the mail from Julian, for the cost of the McDonald's food and the cab fare. I wasn't surprised that he paid me back, and I enjoyed reading his short note about how much he liked his job at the hotel and how he had gotten an apartment nearby with one of his co-workers.

Two years later, I was attending a New Jersey Hotel Business Partnership Event and ran into my hotel friend there. I immediately asked about Julian, and I was elated to discover that he had done extremely well and was now the Assistant Director of Security at the hotel.

Although Julian and I hadn't spoken since the night we met in the train station, I felt compelled to reach out and ask his permission to write about the night we met. I contacted my hotel friend and asked him to forward my number to Julian. It took a few weeks, but eventually Julian called in early 2018. He graciously gave me permission to write this piece, and I am happy to report he is married now and has a family of his own. Although he no longer works in the hotel business, he is a successful security consultant for a Southeastern company.

<u>EDGY</u>

Just like your smile

The morning sun warms me

As your essence stretches across

My heart's skyline

Eclipsing my edginess

SUMMER STASIS

June days just seem longer

Even the wind holds its breath

Caught up in a summer stasis

Children's voices

From across the fence

Drift in damp syllables

Drops of condensation

Create serpentine tracks on foggy glass

And summer is only interrupted

By an occasional discontented sigh

DAMN

Your gaze burns into me

I cannot resist reaching out to you

Placing my hand on the back of your neck

I bring our foreheads together

A flush of warmth rushes through me

As we both lean in …

And then I wake up

WAKE ME UP WHEN SEPTEMBER ENDS

Pain rules over me

As it does every year

On these last days of September

Cracking open this old, dusty, journal

I travel back to a time

When the love notes

You wrote

In the margins

Left me breathless

Vividly I remember

Fingers interlocked

In twisted sheets

Watching the sequined

Stars fade from the

Summer sky

Painting us in dawn's

Blushing glow

We were masters

Of living in the moment

The way you looked at me

With those walnut colored eyes

Made me feel like

Nobody else mattered

I miss that

And I miss you

Because no one

Has made me feel

That important

Since

THE STORM AND YOU

As I sit here on the front porch in the rocker, Mazzy Star's song, "Fade Into You," is on the stereo. I am watching the sky which is an eerie golden color and clouds with different depths of gray color roll overhead. It's becoming dusk so everything is muted with the pale evening glow of dusk giving the entire neighborhood an old sepia toned photo hue. All of the colors are still vivid, however layered with beige variations. The edges of the speckled gray clouds are tinged with a yellow spark.

I look at all of this and think of how much I miss you. I would love to be able to share the gentle breeze which has become cooler and heavier with humidity, but refreshing in its light scent and cool feeling.

The rain has begun to gently fall in great contrast to the public display of lightning and thunder that threatens of heavier showers to come.

Storms seem to bring my innermost thoughts to the surface. It has been this way since I was a young boy. Back then … I used to kneel over the back of the sofa and peer out our front bay window catching every glimpse of a thunderstorm. I remember vividly trying to memorize every detail so I could replay it in my mind later as I drifted off to sleep.

The winds have now ceased and the rain gently increases in

intensity but is still a soft but constantly falling shower.

The glow of the streetlights casts pools of golden brilliance up and down my street. When my eyes begin to close I see your perfect face and drift peacefully off to sleep.

DOES ANYONE HAVE SOME GLUE?

Just like the torn pages of an old book

He tries to fit all of the pieces

Of his heart

Back

Together

THE SHADOW

Dark silence

Validates my presence

Deserted muse

Brashly ignores it

Misty mirror

Reflects

The dark side of light

Wrecked and ragged

Disconnected thoughts

Stab the shadow

Empty echoes answer back

As the rain continues to fall

From the weeping sky

I'LL NEVER BE ENOUGH

When you hold my face in your hands

And kiss me on the forehead

Confusion sets in

The way I feel about you

And the words you do not say

Bring me face to face

With the realization

That I will

              Never

                     Be

                            Enough

<u>DISTANCE</u>

The distance between

Love .... and here

One breath

One look

One touch

ED AND GABBY

He traces the indentations of her soft fingerprints

As his own fingers intertwining

Weave through hers

Their arms in mirroring positions

His canvassed by hers

Like a jigsaw puzzle

With no missing piece

A perfect fit ...

DEREK'S AURA

I still feel him here unseen but ever present. He had an aura that filled the room and made you consciously aware of him. Not from a sense of need or want. There was something about Derek that made you feel better. His simple way and the rapport he had with the young and the old, and his ability to converse in the language of the moment, was astounding.

I would sit back and bask in the penetrating power of his presence.

He possessed a quiet depth of dignity, unflappable, yet always ready to release a laugh resonating from deep within like the sound of the roaring surf in a coastal canyon.

THE CENTER

*Inspired by my best friend, King Kaazi

Embrace each moment

And take some time to sigh

And stop

Be proud of where you have landed

Never forget where your journey began

Because that ... is your center

ETERNAL HEARTBREAK

It's a haunting pattern

The way the moonlight spills

Across the bedroom floor

Fragmented by the window pane

And when the clouds obscure the light

Leaving me and the room

In shadow once again

It gives me a taste

Of all nights to come

Seasoned with the flavor

Of eternal heartbreak

47

9-11

My favorite Ryan Adams song is, "New York, New York," and ironically the music video for this song was filmed three days prior to 9-11. I remember feeling a twinge of sadness when the video was released a few days after 9-11 because the New York City skyline that I had gazed up at in awe since I was a young boy, now had a gaping hole where the twin towers once stood so proudly.

September twelfth was always a somber day for my family because it is the day that Grandma Cozzi died. Additionally, the twelfth of September is my parent's wedding anniversary, but ever since my grandmother's death, it has been a day filled with mixed emotions so my parents usually celebrated on the eleventh or the thirteenth.

For me, the twelfth was always a "bad luck" day so when I was booking my flight to go down to visit my mom and dad, I told my travel agent to book me for September 11th.

I am not a very good traveler. I inherited my mom's "travel nerves." Both of us suffered from butterfly riddled stomachs every time we embarked on a trip, and that wasn't because we were afraid of airplanes or accidents, it was more about us just wanting to get to our destination without any complications. In fact, my biggest fear about flying was getting airsick in public and feeling embarrassed.

The night before my flight on 9-11, I was restless and

agitated. I slept only an hour or so and I remember vividly the dream I had. I dreamt about my late friend, Derek, and he told me in the dream how falling snow sounds very different in heaven and that everything was so much brighter up there and he laughed about having to wear sunglasses. When I woke up, I was definitely a bit more relaxed and I loved that even in death, Derek still had the ability to calm my nerves and make me laugh.

I scribbled down the details of this dream in my journal before making my way to the shower.

My friend, Danni, picked me up that morning to drive me to the airport and I found it interesting that she was experiencing her own nervous stomach. I wonder if we both sensed that something awful was about to happen?

What I recall most about 9-11 is that it was a crystal clear day and the sky was a magnificent shade of blue. I was flying out of terminal C that day and my flight was scheduled to depart at 9:05 am. I called my parents from a pay phone a few minutes before I boarded the plane to let them know that I was departing on schedule because they lived over an hour from Myrtle Beach Airport and they planned on making a few stops on the way.

I typically make sure to have an aisle seat in case I feel sick on the plane, but on this particular day I gave up my aisle seat for a family that wanted to sit together. Hence I had a window seat instead. It was such a clear day that I could see the World Trade Center's twin towers off in the distance. After I put on my Walkman, I looked out the window again and I saw what looked like a smoke stack billowing out of one of the towers. And before I could really digest what I was seeing, the pilot announced that we would be exiting the aircraft. When I got up to the front of the plane, I asked the flight attendant what was happening and she said she didn't know but thought a small private plane may have hit one of the towers.

I immediately ran to the pay phone to call my parents to catch them before they left, but I got their answering machine so I left a message saying that my flight was delayed.

I walked over to the restaurant that was in the terminal and people were already huddled around the television and that is when I realized the magnitude of what had happened. The man next to me was distraught as he frantically tried phoning his wife who worked in one of the towers. His cell phone wasn't getting reception so I pointed him towards the section of pay phones where I had made my calls.

We watched together as the first tower crumbled to the ground. Not long after that, there was an announcement over the PA that the terminal was being evacuated and we were instructed to calmly make our way to the nearest exit, which for us was all the way down the other end of the terminal.

Panic ensued as people began running and tripping over one another. It was a scary and dangerous situation because there were no airport employees present to assist with anything. I don't know if it was my training in emergency procedures from my years working as a hotel manager, but I remained extremely calm. I remember looking across the sea of people and noticing an elderly woman who was standing there frozen in fear. I immediately ran around to one of the gates and grabbed a wheelchair before making my way over to the woman. I introduced myself and told her that we would be getting out of here together. She told me her name was Jessica and that she had arthritis in both of her knees and could not walk very fast.

After getting Jessica settled in the wheelchair, I threw her carry-on bag over my shoulder, running as fast as I could to the end of the terminal and out the exit door.

Once outside, I suggested that we head over to where the police were located, which was a safe distance from Terminal C. I noticed that Jessica also had a Walkman in her bag. I thought that was interesting because Jessica was in her 80's. She smiled and said, "I have to have my music," and I replied, "So do I!" I showed her my Walkman and we immediately dove into this conversation about music. I was trying to find something to talk to her about to keep her calm, and I later found out that she was doing the exact same thing for me.

I was fascinated to discover that Jessica was a retired musician who had played the cello in the New York

Philharmonic for years. She was also a composer who played six different musical instruments and I reveled as she spoke of her adventures living the life as a traveling artist.

I am convinced that Jessica and I were able to survive and get through this horrific day because of our musical connection. It distracted us from the mayhem and kept us calm.

Amid all of the chaos, the airport was eerily silent that day because all planes had been grounded and as I looked across the horizon I could see the white gray smoke rising from where the towers once stood.

Jessica and I heard about Flight 93 crashing in Pennsylvania from the police radio.

I remember giving my handkerchief to a flight attendant who was crying nearby and I will never forget the image of her burying her face in my handkerchief as one of the police officers consoled her as he led her away to sit in his car.

After several hours of waiting outside the terminal, the airport began letting taxi cabs in to pick up all of the stranded passengers. Jessica and I were escorted by a police officer and put in the first taxi to leave Terminal C.

The roads in and around the airport were deserted and even when we made our way onto the highway, there were very few cars and trucks on the road. Our taxi driver had 1010 WINS News Radio and we listened as the events of the day continued to unfold.

When we arrived at my house, Jessica and I exchanged phone numbers and I told her that I would call her later. Once I was inside, I called my mom and dad, Danni, and the rest of my friends and family who had left messages on my answering machine.

The days and weeks that followed are still a blur, but I do remember when baseball returned and watching the games with my friends. Even though the Yankees didn't win the World Series against the Arizona Diamondbacks that year, it remains one of the most memorable for me. The unity that we all felt as Americans in the aftermath of 9-11 was inspiring. Getting back to baseball, our favorite pastime, felt right as we hung American flags outside our front doors and on our cars in solidarity. I miss that and I wish that we had been able to sustain some of the harmony that we found during the 2001 World Series.

The friendship that was born between me and Jessica on that historic day in September was special. Over the years, I was fortunate enough to meet her entire family and hear her play the cello in a symphony concert she did with the local high school students.

Jessica taught me that you must follow your passion and disavow what others might say.

I carry her wise words with me to this day and I know Jessica would be pleased to know that I am now a published author living the life of the artist she told me I was.

THE WISH

A quiet sun drifts in

Dust clings to its sunken rays

Flaws on this old windowsill are visible

Two Adirondack chairs in the corner

Sit unused

Their sloping heads hunched over

Waiting

Quiet and still

The last time you were here

We sat in these chairs

And in that moment

I wished for an eternity …

IMAGINARY KISS

Beyond the white trim

On the square porch windows

Falling rays catch the blue

Of the reflective glass ornament

That wears the John Lennon-esque peace sign

The pages of my journal

Ingest indigo infused sunlight

As it dances toward a twilight slumber

The words I write

Consume the last image I have

Of you silhouetted by the coming dusk

I remember your soft, "I love you"

Whispered above the purr of the retreating tide

Today I wish to linger here

Because when I close my eyes gently

I can taste the salt upon our lips

Giving balance to this imaginary kiss

EVEN THE FISH

Words fall like rain

Into a lake of hopes

Even the fish can't help but dream....

REDDISH KNOB

It was our senior year of college at James Madison University. We had driven up to Reddish Knob, one of the highest peaks in the Shenandoah mountains, to spend one of our last nights together before being separated by our careers and ambitions. I remember writing about this night in my journal after everyone had fallen asleep and all these years later I can read these words and the sights and sounds come rushing back. O

Most of us will not remember the details

Of piling into Chris-Ann's LTD

The car we nicknamed, "The Tank"

Because it fit all seven of us comfortably

(Well, sort of!)

This is the last time we'll take this ride up to Reddish Knob together

A ride we have taken at least twice a month every fall and spring

For the last four years

Our usual spot is located next to an old weeping willow tree at the peak of the mountain

The climb to the top is steep

But we do it now without even having to rest on the way up

Everyone was in good spirits tonight

Because final exams are over for good

We celebrated by drinking beer and

Bartles & Jaymes wine coolers by the fire

That burned in celebration of us

With the realization

That our days of youth were coming to a close

And the future outside of school

That we always saw as so distant

Was tapping on our shoulders

I'll never forget the way the marshmallows smelled

When we put them on the end of sticks and toasted them on the fire

While watching the crimson sun dip below the horizon

Or the burgundy red color of the pipe Dolan smoked

Synthetic dreams out of

Or when Mark played Springsteen's

"Sherry Darling" on his Fender guitar

Just as the sun came up

And we huddled together with our arms around one another

Singing along at the top of our lungs

We'll never forget how we all laughed and sang

And screamed as the Virginia Mountains stood in protection

Of the creatures that brought such vibrations of life

We'll never forget the drunken kisses on eager lips

And we'll never forget about the nights we spent

Running through the vacant streets of Harrisonburg after last call

Dancing to the songs played by our favorite college band, The Spark Plugs

Years from now

We will just look back

At all those familiar strangers

That we once were

And see them

As if they were all standing in front of us

Engulfed by their vulnerability

And now as I think about this night that represented so much of my youth

I yearn for those days when naïve indulgences were plentiful

QUIET DREAMING

The world sits quiet

In here

As I dream

Beyond these walls

HAPPY BIRTHDAY

As another birthday looms on the horizon

I realize this …

The older we get

The less time slows down

I find that it helps to remember

The simpler days

Before all of the chaos that surrounds me now

Invaded my world

I don't want to forget

The simplicity of those early years

Or the post birthday visits to the roller rink with my friends

With my mom and dad chasing our pounding footsteps

Down the long hallway that lead to the skate desk

It was a typical late 1970's joint

Tacky in the daylight

But something much more magical

Beneath strings of bright colored lights

It was under these floodlit colors

Where I held my first hand

And braved my first kiss on a dare at age 13

I am much older now

And I carry on in the ordinary world

But I think I will always live a little

Inside our roller skate tracks

On the maple wood rink floor

Surrounded by animal shaped balloons and disco fries

MY BOLD MOVE

Dotted in white from the lone lamp lighting this library
hallway

Our careful voices skim the crest of silence

We connect over the Michener novel, "The Fires of Spring"

The one you are holding in your hand

I find you so immensely attractive and engaging

That I am compelled to make an

Unusually bold move

And politely ask to see your phone

While offering up a brief smile

Before adding my name and number

To your list of contacts

Putting "Michener library guy" in parenthesis beside my
name

I return your phone and we lock eyes

But nothing is certain

Because I see a mixture of shock and intrigue

Behind those light brown eyes

No other words are spoken

As we depart

So I guess I just have to wait

To see if you text or call

MOVIE NIGHT

"It isn't a date. We are just going to see the new Rocky film together."

This is exactly what I kept repeating to myself

Maybe it was just a coincidence

When we both reached for the armrest

But when your hand touched mine

You didn't pull it away

Choosing instead to keep it on top of mine for a minute

Before removing it

It was hard maintaining my composure

Because I really wanted to hold your hand

For me

Holding hands is the most intimate of gestures

But I know it is too early for something like that

And I have to stop myself

Before I begin imagining what it would feel like

To kiss you goodnight

After all

We only met at the library three weeks ago

And you are still grieving a loss

That made you move 3,000 miles

For a fresh new start

Perhaps there is some truth

To what I wrote in my journal the day we met

About the universe putting us together

Because now that my eyes are open

So is my heart

FRIGHTENED HEART

I keep my adoration for you

In a box

Buried deep

On top of my other secrets

Beside the things too daring to feel or say

Sometimes when you squint at me

I think to myself …

"Wow … I really could love you."

Maybe one day

When the timing is just right

I can tell you

That this frightened heart is yours …

DISCOVERY

Every movement

Feels like a new discovery

We become more at ease

With each intimate gesture

I love how we

Avoid tumbling outside of ourselves

Just to make the other person happy

What a delightful simplicity we have here

Sitting together in silence

Below this old sycamore tree

Nobody knows we are here

So no one intrudes

It is just us and the quiet empty space today

This atmosphere is so undeniably perfect

For two friends evolving into something more

Resting my head comfortably on your shoulder

I inhale the sweet scent of fall

Imagining our first kiss

Sometimes I think that the universe

Identified this love

Before we were aware of its existence

NIGHT BIRDS

The night birds

Sing their serenade

To the moon and stars and me

Awakening the silent darkness

Each note

Just right

Each phrase, each harmony

Blending into perfect resonance

Without the need of a conductor's score

They sing effortlessly

Pouring out each note

As if it may be their last

72

I lie here

Alone in the darkness

Listening

With a touch of envy at the sense of companionship

They have with each other

And with their song

ABLAZE

When I look over at you

Our eyes make desperate love

And our hearts beat wildly

From just being near

We are so reserved

Sitting here

Among your family

Knowing that

A single touch

Will set us ablaze ...

THE BETRAYAL

The hallways blur as he walks faster

Away from the wide-eyed face

Of the one he thought would never hurt him

The apologies are bits of glass

That he deflects with his hands

And they spread like stars over his eyes

A betrayal so sudden and cold

Like a knife wound on his skin

A pain so deep it takes a while to rise to the surface

It's in a secluded corner

Of the Princeton Barnes and Nobles

Filled with the gentle whisper of pages turning

And stories unfolding

That he finally allows himself to cry

TAKE ME BACK

Time drips

Like the melting ice

On a shivering branch

Elusively running

Away from you and me

Moments become hours

Days turn into weeks

Then years ... so suddenly

Making me tremble with desire

I need those moments back

When you dreamt of me

In illuminating colors

My head on your chest

Feeling every heartbeat

Do you still smile when you think of me?

Because I do … every time

Now, I am alone

Deep in the middle of the night

Covered in nothing but a yearning desire

I wait for your touch

To seep into my dreams

THE ACTOR

Concealed by shadows

He smiles

    Through

        The

            Pain

SUNSET

Inspired by the b.c.Hudalla poem, "Journey to the Dawn"

Shadows fall into darkness

Undauntedly

Forcing days' end

Having no recourse

But one last stance

Revealing beauty with elegant majesty

The sun gives its own epitaph

THE SHOW

The show was brilliant. It could not have been scripted better, if it had been written by a professional playwright. The shiftiness, nervous twitches, and sad looks were all on cue. She sat with arms crossed, her face blank. Her usual soft blue eyes were now hard and angry, as she tried to keep her hurt covered. An attentive audience could have seen beyond the mask, but not this leading man. He was busy with his own mask. His feigned boyish grins and apologetic face was betrayed by how he held his mouth. That was one trait he had never mastered through the years, as she'd listened to his excuses.

His answers to her questions were all lies, or mostly so. As he spoke, he never touched her once, but his words pierced through her heart, as deeply as any sword could have. Still, she followed the script, and said her lines.

After all was said, the door shut behind him, as he left the stage. His scene was over, and she was alone, with no applause. There was no cheering section. She sat stoic,

listening to be sure he was really gone. Only then did she allow her tears freedom, as she cast herself onto her lonely bed. The curtain had fallen, and it was the end of a long, hard marriage. Now, all that was left for her was to face the ugly reviews.

ONE MOMENT

In this lifetime

Everyone gets a moment

One

Solitary

Special

Moment

When it all comes together just right

And everything swims to the center

Of your heart

Allowing you to be the one

Having the best time in the whole world

With the one you love

And the one who loves you the most

YOUR CANVAS

Life is a canvas

So paint each day

With your written words

Be brave enough to

Send them out into the universe

And every now and then

Stand back and appreciate the lives they touch

"PRETTY WHEN YOU CRY"

The dreamy music of Lana Del Rey

Plays softly on my iPod

I can feel her heart

Beating beneath her lyrics

This old porch rocking chair

Sways gently

Back and forth

Whispering

Lana's half-awake secrets

To the chilly October rain

GETTING IT ALL DOWN

It is in here

Between empty circles in time

Where I sit

Writing

Trying feverishly to get it all down on paper

Before the walls of creativity

Begin

To slowly

Close in

I'M DONE WITH YOU

Wringing my hands of love

My heart is nothing but a window painted shut

CHILDHOOD FRIENDS

When I walked past the park earlier

I was reminded of the last time you visited

It had been unseasonably warm that October

The day we walked over to the park together

It was empty except for a mom and a little boy playing in the sandbox

We sat on the swings and rocked lazily

Until you began to really swing

Of course I had to go higher than you

And for just a moment

We were kids again

Laughing and soaring in the air

Innocent and free from worries

Eventually we slowed down

Tangling our chains together

We sat side by side

Feet in the dirt

I look at the ground and laugh

Amazed that

I still feel at my best when I am with you

<u>HAUNTED</u>

Instead of delving into deep wonders together

And pulling things from within our minds that we hadn't yet imagined

You chose to become a ghost

Disillusionment consumes me

Every edge digs sharply

Deepens as I breathe

Haunts me as I close my eyes...

UNREST

In a moment of unrest

The distance appears longer

For a heart that aches

MY BACK DOOR

I loved the way

You expertly

Tore down

The walls

I had built around my heart

Everything felt so much lighter

Until you ghosted me

Then I rebuilt the walls

Making them even taller

I mixed your cowardice as the cement

And used your pretense as the bricks

Eliminating a place to enter

Apart from the back door I inserted

That only the most determined will find

LOVE REMEMBERED

Happy times spent with you

Are sleeping in my memory

But I don't dare disturb their slumber

BLISS

For years

These emotions

Lie still

Eroding and unused

But now they are canvassing a shifting mind

And falling feverishly

Into

Uncharted bliss

FOR MARILYN HAFLER

No ghosts will linger

In the places we have dwelled

For we have loved hard

And what we leave behind

Will be nothing more

Than melodic whispers

Drifting on a breeze

CLOUDS

The clouds write a story

 Moving with the wind

Changing form and color

Without effort

Adapting to unseen forces

Absorbing

Then releasing

Sometimes violently

Thrashing with electricity

Sometimes quietly

With soft tears

And when the sun shines

They move along

 Acclimated

 Accepting

 Just like us

LIFE IN THE SKY

As skies rupture

Air filling with freshness

Nursing plant and tree

Cleansing in preparation

Mirror on the ground

Formed by tears of joy

The passing of the storm

Wades through heart and soul

New creation

Shortly unfurling

Life ...reoccurring

HOW MUCH?

I promised myself

That I wouldn't discuss

The love I have for you

Unless it was completely gone

And here I am

Curled up under my blanket of hearts

Writing about you

So I suppose this love still exists

I do miss the way

You'd hold your smile

When I spoke to you tenderly

And our lengthy phone conversations

That had both of our ears

Red and sore

I miss your Spanish accent

That you exaggerated for me

And your robust laughter

When I tickled you

I miss our opposite tastes in films too

And how you sat through, "The Red Violin"

For me

And how I sat through, "Ironman"

For you

I miss us reading Lewis Carroll aloud to one another

As we snuggled up in bed

Until both of our eyes

Were too heavy to go on

These days, though

I read everything

Silently

And alone

So ... I guess I miss you

Part of me is still yours

And that makes me wonder

How much of yours am I?

<u>WONDER</u>

Childlike dreams

Kiss away

The darkness

Carrying wonder

In each wisp

I GUESS I NEVER REALLY KNEW YOU

Your question stole my breath

The answer was obvious to me

When we reconnected

After so many formidable years

You decided

I needed to be exactly the same as I had always been

In your eyes

I was not supposed to change

But I did

And now you question its authenticity

Because you weren't here to witness any of it

So to you

It is suddenly this major affront?

I guess I never really knew you either

THE KISS

The brittle night air greets us

As we step out of the limo

It is probably 15 degrees

Kind of cold for December

On Lake Tahoe

I can see my breath

And the night air easily permeates our bones

You run off toward the sand

Dressed in your formal attire

I run after you, still in my tuxedo

The sand is hard and nearly frozen under my feet

There are no lights illuminating the beach

104

But the bright moon

Gives us just enough light

For a most memorable New Year's Eve kiss

THE KISS-Part 2

The limo ride to the Lake Tahoe house was quiet

I smiled in silence

Playing back the kiss on the frozen sand

I felt your eyes on me

There was something there

Obviously

Inside that moment

Time stood still

My heart pulsed wildly

When you inched closer

We held hands

Talking intermittently

106

In between some pleasant silences

It was nice that we could be quiet together

And still feel comfortable

For me

This is just as important as a meaningful conversation

The sky looked violet

And like a spotlight on a stage

It lit everything just right

Later on

I wrote like a madman in my journal

Wanting to remember everything about you

And this night

MY ONLY DESIRE WAS TRYING

I almost stumble when I notice you

A lofty familiar face

In the crowd

My cheeks flare up flaming red

Race car of emotions

Drive through

My butterfly stomach

Concealing glances

Filter through the rain

Spilling honesty

On a set of eyes

Pinpricks of clarity

Trickle through

Making me realize

That my only desire was trying

THE MASTERPIECE

I am looking for someone

Who writes music

On my heart

And dances

While washing the dishes

Long after they are spotless

Because the song

Is not over

I am looking for someone

Who knows that some words can move mountains

Opening doors on walls

That forgot that doors were ever there

I am looking for someone

Who knows

Sometimes

No words are needed

I look forward

To memorizing your face

And composing the masterpiece

That neither of us

Can write alone …

JOY

Tender expressions

A soliloquy unspoken

Reflects joy in a pair of eyes

Moments treasured

A smile imprinted forever

On the others' heart

WRITER

Words tumble from my mind

Like the color

From a fading photograph

Alone against a memory

STRENGTH

For Danni and Chayce

Standing back up after all the pain

Thoughts of warmth and love rejuvenate your spirit

Remembering the special moments that made these memories

Every day you still go on

Nothing stands in your way

Grateful for all you still have

Thoughts racing, hope rising

Heartache falling away

SUNBEAMS ON THE WATER

Sun drops in

Softly at first

Beam after beam

Dancing atop the

Thirsty blue green ocean water

UNREACHABLE

Sitting on the back porch

Out of sight and writing down verses

His heart is unreachable

For it belongs to one

Whose heart is already full ...

WINTER MELANCHOLY

Sun kissed tears

Fall all along

The icy pond

While the frosted willow tree

Quietly weeps

For summer's return ...

THE ACCIDENT

The pavement stares up at me

My eyes want to look ahead

But the path is scary

Sirens in the distance

Speak of mayhem

I reach for my phone

Thrown across the car on impact

And the first thing I see

Is your beautiful face

Somehow my pictures gallery opened

And your face was the first thing I saw

I have never been so thankful to see those eyes

118

A child's voice behind me

Speaks of warmth

The breeze kisses me softly

A strong hand takes my own

I raise my eyes

And look before me

Grateful to be alive

UNINVITED

The last time

You appeared in my dreams

Uninvited

Was 15 years ago

I used to try and write about you

And the way you looked at me

When you were proud

And the way you lovingly brushed the hair

From my forehead

Now

You are only fragments

That are just

Too far away

To touch ...

A SEA OF SILENCE

Your few words drowned

In a sea of silence

That lingered above me

As I stared up at the bedroom ceiling

I am tired of wondering where I faltered

So I let myself fall back under

The comforter of hurt hearts

And wait silently for

The next chapter to begin

IN THE MIDST OF DEVASTATION

He defied all

And fought with all his might

He glowed from the drops

Of the morning's first rain

Weak ...

But determined

To uncover something beautiful

In the midst

Of such devastation

LIFE

Life is a series of moments

Interconnected

Like the links of a chain

Strung together

One after another

Some are fleeting

Other linger

They make up our experiences

Which

In turn

Make our life whole

There are:

Moments of comfort

Moments of excitement

124

Moments of sadness

Moments of joy

Moments of pain

Moments of ecstasy

Moments to cherish

And then ...

Some moments are finite

Some radiate through a life

Becoming faded, distant memories

But ...

The perfect moments

Are easily recalled

In textbook clarity

As if they just happened today

And they remain

The most precious

CREATIVELY INSPIRED

Bridging the gaps

We drift into the future

With a purpose

Moving forward

Creatively inspired

Flowing seamlessly

Together

With wide open hearts

OVER AND OVER

Night has fallen

And sidles up

Closely around us

Your darkness and mine

Enfolding us

My thoughts are of you

As my smile breaks free

And you fill my head

Like a favorite song

Put on repeat

Over and over …

PETER CINCOTTI

*Inspired by the song, "Roman Skies."

You strike the keys of the piano

Releasing energy and hope

Fingers gently play

Evoked by good intentions

Your melody is a flawless composition

Your timing is perfection as it flows

Soothing and enticing

Demanding and releasing

You play with wild abandon

Convincing no one, least of all yourself

That you are in control of your compulsion

But then a shift in tempo

And the melody takes over

Drowning out the voices of your preconceptions

You cannot stop

The rhythm is mesmerizing

So you let go and follow

Losing decorum …

REFLECTIONS

Sun sets over sand

Shells perfect and imperfect

Reflection of life

TOWING IN THE TIDE OF SLEEP

In his chamber at night

He is sleepless

Reading

Writing

His mind is a spotlight

On an empty stage

Next to him

Books are stacked like stairs

Somewhere

Between the lines

His eyes finally go dark

And his head drops onto the pillow

While the porch light

Gently tows in

The tide of sleep

INNER ECHO

Our lives echo

A silent voice

That whispers inside our minds

Storing our memories

And packaging our joys and sorrows

Releasing reminders

Of precious moments

That attach to our hearts

Forever

WORDS FROM A COMPLEX HEART

The words were trapped

Inside your deepest breathe

Until

You breathed new life

Into my atmosphere

By voicing this simple phrase

From your complex heart:

"I love you"

<sigh>

134

RIDE

Between the moon and me

My dreams are unearthed

Secrets unwind

As I lay down my head

Hoping that your presence will appear

And whisk me away

To ride high above the clouds

<u>QUESTIONS</u>

What if we met at a different time and different place?
Would our lives still take us on separate but intersecting paths
or would we find each other and be together?

What if money didn't matter? Would that change your
priorities enough making people come first?

What if you allowed yourself to be happy? Would you
believe that you deserve that instead of punishing yourself
over and over again?

What if you were to let go of the past and look at the world
with fresh eyes ...would you allow yourself the freedom to
love again and embrace it?

What if you knew how sad you sometimes make me feel?
Would you really mean it when you say you're sorry?

What if I told you I love you? Would that change anything at
all?

136

BREAKTHROUGH

In the core of everything

There is a breakthrough in the unseen

A light

And hope

Hidden between the lines

FEELINGS RISE BACK TO THE SURFACE

I tried to leave the memory of you behind me

But I woke up with your image still in sight

Sometimes I hate when old feelings

Travel back and invade the heart again

I really don't mind all that much

Being alone

But part of me now

Just wants to be where you are

Wherever that is

But I can't

So instead

I am reaching out with every word I write

Hoping they make it to you

So your eyes can see

How much I miss you

And wish that you were here

139

RAIN DRENCHED THOUGHTS

The silence is poking me in the ear

A cloudburst of thoughts bring me here

Giving shape to the feelings

That each of my rain drenched thoughts evoke

140

DISCONNECTED

Whispered words

Leave questions unanswered

While lonely tones

Within the silence

Expose the depth

Of our disconnection

FOUR MONTHS

When my eyes saw you in the multitude of crowds, I recognized you instantly, you stood out from the rest and when you returned my glance I felt both supremely elated and a bit frightened by the beautiful intensity of your dark mysterious eyes.

Your hand brushed up accidentally against mine. Already I felt lost in the future embrace of yours arms.

"You found me in the midst of confusion." I remember telling you on our first date, but now, four months later everything had changed and we were standing outside at the airport saying good bye.

The breeze gently swayed around your hair; and your deep set dark eyes began to tear from the wind.

"You know it wasn't an easy decision... for me," you spoke softly.

I nodded wordlessly, overcome with emotion.

"What if..." I commenced a sentence of wondrous possibilities that was left hanging in the air, unfinished, quivering.

"We can't think about that now. It's important to be patient, to wait and see...

Those had been my words. I always speak wise words before an impending catastrophe; wise words to protect me from eventual possible disaster. Wait and see...

I guess you were attracted to me. Your definition of love was different than mine. You had left behind your country and your ex-lover. And now you were returning to both.

We stood there in awkward silence, both lost in the train of our thoughts. Each of us had parallel dreams that lived side by side, not merging.

The moment to part was coming closer.

We stood there for a long, long time. People were rushing around us, past us, with their suitcases and luggage in hand, their boarding passes and their indicated destinations. And still we stood there. Frozen

I had to let you go, so I gave you a hurried hug, and turned around slowly, detaching myself from your eyes. I walked away from you, with the faint hope that you would maybe call out my name.

BRUISED HEART

This heart

Isn't lonely

It's just

A little black and blue

TWO PARTS

Our bodies fit together

As if they were torn from one another

Leaving no cracks

Your silhouette curves with mine

The passionately systematic method

In which we love

Has convinced me of this theory

That we are two parts

Of the same soul

<u>TOO CLOSE</u>

You were made of light and heat

And held the most illuminating brightness

A glowing flame of sorts

But I got too close

At the wrong moment

WILL YOU ...

Will you miss me after I am gone when you hear a familiar
song playing on the radio?

And the melody and chorus follow you wherever you go?

Will you be filled with regret when you see me on the street
walking toward you on a blustery fall day?

When you see that smile again knowing what could have
been?

WILL YOU? (Part Two)

Will you love me if I share with you all of my dreams, my successes, and my failures?

When I am at the top of my game … and when I am not?

Will you love me when my lips meet yours and I wrap my arms around you?

Or when you wake in the morning and watch me as I sleep?

148

THE SECRET LANGUAGE

He's the only one who ever understood. He would walk in and find me sitting there …listening …and he wouldn't ask. He'd just sit down with me on the floor and listen until he figured it out.

I feel the music. It becomes a part of me and me a part of it. Everything in my mind melts into the words and notes.

And he understood.

He would be the one to pull me back to reality and away from the music.

It was all unspoken.

No one ever said a thing.

The music did my talking and he was the only one who knew the language.

EYES OPEN

With open eyes

Our damaged hearts

Become more hopeful

As we fill each other in

DOG TAG

It was Saturday, August 8, 2015. I woke up around 8am having dreamt about my friend, Derek, the night before. Waking up to the reminder that he was still gone had my head and my heart reeling. Grief is like that. It comes at us in full force no matter how many years have gone by since we lost our loved one.

I was happy it was the weekend and I didn't have to work because I desperately needed an, "alone day."

As I placed my red tea kettle on the stove for my morning bowl of oatmeal, I plugged my iPod into myBose stereo and chose Bruce Springsteen's "Born to Run" record as the soundtrack for my morning. This is an album that Derek and I both loved and we knew every lyric and every instrumental beat by heart. Each time I listen to any of these tracks, I am immediately transported back to a time when he and I were together singing our faces off and nothing else mattered.

I add in a splash of half and half to my plain oatmeal and I laugh out loud a little remembering how Derek thought it was quirky of me to eat oatmeal at all times of the day. He was especially disturbed when I would make a bowl of hot oatmeal on a 100 degree summer day! He found it so interesting that I had no trouble adding half and half or milk to my oatmeal, but I could not bear to put milk on regular cereal, choosing instead to eat it dry.

Admittedly, I was the quirky one in this relationship.

Not many would have put the two of us together. It is like
that for me and so many of my friends. I am not sure why
people have such a preconceived idea about the type of
friends I should have. It has been this way from for as long as
I can remember. Maybe it is because my closest friends are
usually polar opposites of sorts. Either way, I have never
given much thought to the opinions of others. I like who I
like … period!

Anyone who has ever been in my house knows how deeply I
admire and love the music of Stevie Nicks and Fleetwood
Mac. Derek was not a fan before becoming my friend, but he
grew to appreciate Stevie's music and the music of Fleetwood
Mac. Derek loved, "Rhiannon," and when the Fleetwood
Mac album, "The Dance," came out in early 1997, he fell in
love with that particular live version of the song. He liked
that it began slowly and softly with just Christine McVie
playing the piano and Stevie's voice before the ever so
familiar guitar riffs kicked off the most recognizable part of
the song.

Months later, Derek asked me to play this version of
"Rhiannon" for him as he waited patiently in his hospital bed
for the nurse to take him over to radiology for a CT scan.
Two hours earlier, I had taken him here to, New York
Presbyterian Hospital, because I was extremely concerned
about the piercing headaches he had been getting. They
never lasted very long, but the pain was excruciating. I could

tell that he was scared and so was I, but as I held his hand while "Rhiannon" played on my Walkman, I felt both of our fears subside a bit. And when the nurse wheeled him away for the CT scan, he was more relaxed and I felt a bit more hopeful as well.

I was not at all prepared when the doctor come up to me in the waiting room with the news that Derek had died during the scan. I was literally frozen in that moment and only remember hearing the words "cerebral hemorrhage" and that Derek died instantly.

I could not believe that my best friend was gone, He was only 28.

A few weeks after Derek's death, I was given a box containing some of his personal belongings. Over the years, I have gone through some of the contents of this box, but I've never been able to look at more than one or two things at a time.

On that Saturday in August of 2015, I revisited Derek's box and found a small gift box that had a silver bow on it that must have been a gift he had purchased for someone. I hesitated for a moment, thinking that it was probably a gift for the fiancé he left behind, but I decided to open it anyway. Inside the gift box, I was shocked to find a beautiful silver dog tag necklace engraved with, "Forever Friends: Derek and Robert." He must have had this made for my birthday the year he died. My eyes welled up with tears as I held it in my hands. Our favorite Springsteen song was "Backstreets" so the, "forever friends," comes from the line in that song: "We swore forever friends, on the backstreets until the end."

I remember running upstairs and immediately calling my mom in North Carolina to tell her what I had just found and I will never forget what she wrote on my Facebook page after I posted about my discovery. She said, "If people are lucky they will have in their lifetime one good friend like Derek. My heart aches for you with this loss that has so affected your life, but I think Derek is proud of the man you have become. He was the brother you didn't have and you will always remember him when others have simply moved on and left him behind."

This gift that sat in Derek's box for eighteen years is now something I wear around my neck every day. And maybe I was meant to find it when I did, on a day when I felt especially sad and alone. The thought of Derek orchestrating all of this is not outside the realm of possibility.

Sometimes my television turns on by itself. To be clear, I am not usually a believer in such things but it has happened with every television I have owned since Derek's death, so maybe this is just another way of letting me know that his presence still lingers here.

I kind of like the idea of that …

ETERNALLY

We try to be brave

And strong

And good

We do the right thing

But at night

We haunt one another's dreams.

I hope you read this

For I know you're out there

Somewhere

Watching me from afar

Making sure I'm okay

Your heart is sewn to mine

Forever

WHISPERED WORDS

My words whisper in your ears

Touching your spirit

While silk strands of imagination

Silence our fears

BOND

Tonight

Although separated

We are two beating hearts

Dreaming in unison

Under the same dark November sky

THE BLUE LAMP

The room is

Set apart

Cold … with one lone blue lamp burning

A reminder of life

Love

And smiles that lit your eyes

With mischievous teasing

Life lessons hidden

Behind faded blue

Briefly revealed

Learned together

Now …

One remains alone

To guard the lamp

And tend to the empty room

GUITAR

Inspired by Jamie Lamarra

Gently strum my strings

Under my neck and

I will sing for you

Take me strapped upon your back

And I will follow and help you

Reach your dreams

THE WARMTH OF A TOUCH

Like sand castles at high tide reaching out

Anxious for the water to touch their edges and free them

I too reach out to you

For the warmth of your fingers laced with mine

THE STILLNESS OF REMEMBERING

A quiet sun drifts in

Dust clings to its sunken rays

Flaws in this old windowsill are visible

Two Adirondack chairs in the corner

Sit unused

Their sloping backs hunched over

Waiting

Quiet and still

The last time you were here

We sat in these chairs

And in that moment

I wished for an eternity

162

INTOXICATING MOMENT

Our racing heartbeats

And muted giggles

Echo from

This flower-laden rooftop

Your face

Iridescent upon

The orange sunlight

That floods this black and white tiled floor

Pieces of you

Reside in the melodies

Of the delicate songs

Playing from the stereo

163

My camera

Records the quaint beauty

Of solitude

That roams listlessly

Around this picturesque rooftop garden

Today

We are two lovers lost

In a lingering

Intoxicating moment

AWAKENED HEART

After we kiss

My heart

Is no longer

Deserted

A pinprick of light

Enters the deep blue darkness

Allowing me

To remember

Exactly how

Passion feels

<u>RETURNING SOLDIER</u>

He sits alone

On this grey October day

Back up against the door

Protecting his solitude

When he came home from Afghanistan

He didn't expect to land here

In a rooming house

With strangers

The loved ones in the pictures

He kept inside his helmet

Were nowhere to be found

Everyone had moved on

Without him

The very thought of this

Has him nervously scratching

His thumb nail

On the wall

Adjacent to the door

And as he digs into

Its ghostly surface

He sees

Underneath the plain

And tired faded white

That suffocates the room

Someone

Who liked the color blue

167

HOPES AND WISHES

We all eagerly anticipate

The dawning of a brand new day

Because it brings

New hopes

For unfulfilled wishes

Lying dormant within our hearts

Instilling and awakening

Fresh new desires

That will lead us to

A new veracity

ARTISTIC HEARTS

When we are together

I feel perfect

I wonder if this is destiny

Or the result of ardent striving on my part?

Maybe it's just life's course

Controlled by the rhythm of time's tumblers?

Nah …

I prefer to think of it as a collision of two artistic hearts

SURROUNDED BY CHAOS

*Inspired by Jon Foreman

Sometimes I feel like

I am chasing an illusion

Because

Occasionally

I sit languidly

Amidst all of the chaos

Tranquilly indecisive

But that is just how I like it

Sometimes …

LONESOME SILENCE

A new day begins

Where my memory resides

Surrounded by an understanding

I struggle to find

Heart at my sleeve

Searching for a glimpse of light in the shadows

And a comforting whisper

In the lonesome silence

PERFECTLY WRITTEN SONGS

A thousand feelings

Rush in

As I hang on to the melodies

In perfectly written songs

My heart still swells

Insatiably

A wistful sigh

Passes through my stillness

When I remember exactly

How it feels

To be in love …

<u>BROKENHEARTED</u>

There are no words

That can adequately define

The hole in my heart today …

RESILIENCE

Their pain is bitter

It lays there like a blanket of thorns

Soft on the outside

Sharp and cutting on the inside

I can feel their hearts

Their aches and forced smiles

Wilting softly from within

But I can feel their resilience building too

Because everything they dreamed of

And

Longed for

Is so much stronger than all of the pain

SECRET GARDEN

I sit propped up

On the chaise lounge

Near the end of the beach

At the edge of the boardwalk

Books in hand, writing tablet to my side

Bundled up in a comfy sweatshirt

On this late September day

In the Distance

Bright pieces of sea glass reflect on the sand

White caps dance atop the rolling surf

I close my eyes

Breathing deep to the count of ten

175

Panic and anxiety

Is replaced

With calm

Solitude abounds

Providing inspiration and peace

Unseen and hidden out of sight

Reading novels and writing down verses

This is my "secret garden"

FRACTURED HEARTS

Emotions pass by

Sometimes colliding

Within an inch

Of ravenous minds

Inches we save

Become emotions

Denied

That echo in between

Galaxies and hallucinations

But someone's love

Can be the glue

For these fractured hearts

177

LOST IN THE HAZE

Your words come in spurts

After a pause for thought

Or maybe it's just effect

Falling from your lips

Like soft rain drops

I know you believe

But these words of yours are a paradox

Clarity is not lost in the haze

Gravity is not to blame

For pulling us apart

Or bringing us back together

These walls of yours keep you safe

No ladder high enough

No bridge long enough

Fingers stretched out

Needing to hold on

Gasping for air

And your eyes, those beautiful eyes

They reveal the truth

Even as you look away

CONVERSATION

This is not the first time I have had this conversation

With you

I am trying to get it right

As if right could ever exist between us

SPACES

I am the

Spaces

Between books

On a dark shelf

CHEATER

It would have been easier

If he had never seen you

Secretly kissing another

So he hides his face

From the light of the room

Relying on the kitchen wall to hold him up

Feeling as if the sharpest knife he owns

Is painstakingly slicing his heart piece by piece

CONDITIONAL LOVE

Years ago

I fell for you

I still remember how my hands would shake whenever you
spoke to me

I could not control them

And that is when I knew I was doomed

For if I could not control my hands

How in the world would I control my heart?

And I was right

Because you let me love you

Until you decided it was time for a change

So …

There I was

Watching you wave goodbye to me

183

From the train platform

Knowing that you were never coming back

Thinking about you now

Makes me wonder

Do you make his hands shake when you talk to him like you did mine?

A BEAUTIFUL TRAP

I look into your eyes

And I see the moon

I'd like to travel

Back and forth

Trapped in your reflection

THE EXPLORER

It's in the very darkness

Where you'll find the silence

Many times it is welcoming

Other times it is deafening

Untouched waters run deep

It's where discovery can begin

And real understanding awaits

It's the one explorer

Who is pure of heart and mind

Who can hold the sun

In the very dark of night

Prodding carefully

Gentleness of touch

Blades placed away safely

Respecting this life

It's the yearning for more

The ability to comprehend

The desire for compassion

The need for love

So we find a way

A PRACTICE OF HOPE

This love

Rises from a concealed horizon

Lofty clouds disperse

To thoughts of when and how

Blazoned and ensued

By the practice of hope

BEGINNINGS

A new beginning

Breathes fresh in my air

Carelessly floating

Daring me to hope

And eager to grasp

But…

Fears old and new

Grow out of past hurts

Memories too new to die

Now new beginnings

Open doors for me

Helping to

Put the past finally to rest

Quietly and alone

I take a step forward

THE STORY

What if my story

begins

the moment

I break free

from this one?

LANA DEL REY

Friday night

Low lights and melodic grooves

The tempo of a memory

Vibe stolen from a dream

The music makers

Thank you, Lana

ONE

I fit perfectly

Into the recesses of you

Slipping between

Tongue

Cheek

And groove

We are sleek perfection

One …

FLEETING THOUGHTS

Tonight the thoughts come and go

Like winter waves on an icy shore

Back and forth

Some sling on to my deeper insight

Others toss and turn

Between words

I choose to ignore

The ones that try to pull me under

So I remind myself to breathe

Until nostalgia's familiar melody

Echoes in my ears

DEPTH

The depth of your eyes

Dare me to glance

And the image I see residing there

Matches my dreams

WE ARE EACH OTHER'S ONLY RELEASE

Last night

Your chest was my pillow

As we dozed on the sofa

Together we possess a comfortable strength

That transcends devotion

In every way

We are each other's only release

And even when this irritating voice inside my head

Reminds me

That you are moving away

The dreams we have together

Have no design to ever bring us down

DARK BROWN EYES OF PURE LOVE

When I think of you

I feel your tender fingers laced with mine

I taste your soft lips pressed against my own

I see your face smiling at me

With dark brown eyes of pure love

Making my heart suddenly feel

More alive than ever

DREAMING BEYOND THE LEDGE

Inspired by my best friend, King Kaazi

If you understand what drives me

Then you can know me

If you see into my heart and mind

You can safely claim power over my dreams

If I allow you a glimpse into what I really believe

Perhaps we can empower one another

To jump beyond ourselves

And just like the waterfall

That meets its reflection at the surface

Together we can remind the world

What it is like to dream beyond the ledge

SAN GENNARO 2009

The cymbals crash

The drum rolls

Desire streams in

As voices descend from the night sky

And life's mystical parade

Trumpets down the narrow streets

Of Little Italy

On this San Gennaro evening

Emotions are risked

By unmasked lovers

Escaping the crowd

Once their eyes meet

Each breath invites

Another kiss

A testament

That love has its reasons …

MORE SIGNS

I love how I can close my eyes

And see ...

Laughter spilling from your lips

And your sexy smile

That I trace with my fingertips

Draws me in close

For a prolonged kiss

When I open my eyes

All the unraveled words

Once again

Become the poetry

On this page

More signs

That a magnificent adventure

Is on the edge

Of happening

IN BETWEEN

Every night

Two tangled hearts

Share adoration

So with dedicated longing

They try to reach

New heights of knowing

In between the distance

<u>BREATHE</u>

When talking does not seem to help

And when all of your written words

Lead you right back to the pain

Take time to remember

And allow the silence of the room

To fill your inner peace

MRS. HEALY

Night arrives early again

Falling like stone

This loss has chased away the sun

And swallowed the dawn

Winter's long moon

Has claimed their beloved mother

As spirits weep in candlelit rooms

Wilting softly from within

But aches become joy

When memories are shared

And a mother's everlasting love is realized

205

DRAINED WORDS

Silent words

Scream across his pages

Showing how his heart

Holds his biggest dreams

And his greatest nightmares

Once his pen is drained

He allows his fears

To quietly melt into the darkness

NEW YEAR'S EVE

When I ask you

About New Year's Eve

You just you smile at me

And I don't know where to look

My face feels hot and I know it must be red

I am not sure how to escape from this awkwardness

So I keep silent

But you keep smiling instead of being normal

And giving me an answer

You finally nod and say, "I guess dinner and a game or two of Scrabble would be fun."

And just like that

I am matching your smile with my own

It's pulling painfully on my cheeks

Yet I can't figure out how to stop it

I'm off-balance

And I am not entirely sure

What it is I am going through in this moment

But whatever it is

I kind of like it …

WUTHERING HEIGHTS

Bronte …

Ease my mind will you

Let me disappear between your words

So I can remember the best parts

Of being in love

Once I revisit

Cathy and Heathcliff's Gothic love story

I can't help but think of you and me

Because

When we were in love

We read "Wuthering Heights" to one another in bed

A chapter at a time

Like Cathy and Heathcliff

Neither one of us was prepared

To hit the dead end

That ushered in our demise

To this day

You are in my blood

Just as Cathy

Is in Heathcliff's

Instinctively

BLISSFULLY TORMENTED

Frosted dew from the grass

Blankets the fronts of my sneakers

You are drumming out a beat

Absentmindedly

On the side of your leg

When I reach you

At our agreed meeting spot

In front of the library

I gently tap your headphones

And you offer an expanded version

Of the smile you gave me yesterday

Your hand instinctively reaches for my shoulder

And I am blissfully tormented by your teasing touch

211

<u>SO RIGHT</u>

When you smile

Your mouth creates intricate outlines

Across your cheeks

That remind me of ripples of water

Everything about you is so right

I don't even know

How to properly describe it

But each time I see you smile

It short circuits

Every little piece

Of my heart

HOPE REBORN

Hope brightened

His angst ridden shadows

When your love

Began

Wrapping judiciously around him

DANCING SOULS

The closeness they feel

Is so delectably

Pleasing

The moment

Their two souls

Begin to dance

ENCOUNTER

Basking in the frill of anonymity

We kissed

And suddenly our fears melted away

Intimate emotions

In a dimly lit room

Can be such a predictable promise

Making no concession with your heart

I turned away

And didn't look back

Until I reached the exit

THE WAY YOU MAKE ME FEEL

You bring heaven

To this old library

Spilling fiery charm

Each time I see you

Your words

Vibrate throughout my veins

Like unseen storms

Raging through my heart

WHAT I LOVE ABOUT YOU

I love

How your arms

Are more powerful than words

And how your kiss

More than meets my quotient

THE HEALING POWER OF MUSIC

The music is soft and gentle

And it echoes around the house

Leaping from the floor

To the ceiling

In an instant

Before returning

To the pair of ears

That need it the most

SLEEPING NEXT TO YOU

Learning the language of your lips

They speak to me

Phantom kisses

Felt while sleeping

Have carried me here

Through my dreams

And back to you

219

THE CANDLE

I light my candle

Melting it clear

The air whispers through my bedroom window

My candle burns-blue-white-yellow

I keep it going late into the evening

Sometimes it flickers

Moving torrid patterns

Circling

Tattering

The sparkling flame wanes

Then rises up

Springing form from what you thought was gone

It keeps on fighting

Melting wax as time goes by

Tonight …

The candle is my muse

And

A reflection of me

COFFEE FOR TWO

Inside

The coffee aroma lingers

While the light of the day dozes

Behind closed doors

Your eyes mix into mine

Like a frothy swirl

Our eyes sip

Each other carefully

Making our two hearts chime

FOREVER

When I open my eyes

The morning light is blinding

But your smile brought me here

And pulled me through forever

A COLLAGE OF FACES

I have just arrived at the Sunset Diner, which is one of my favorite places to go for any meal.. The diner is packed so I grab a seat at the counter while I wait for my friend Nick to arrive. I sit and watch the people...a collage of faces. I listen to the hum of conversations interspersed with the clanking of silverware and the shuffle of feet of people passing by. All of this reminds me of discreetly taken photographs and how they capture a moment in time...indecipherable to the casual observer.

I wonder if someone was observing us during my last visit here with Nicholas .We both broke out into uncontrollable laughter when he was telling me about how his dog, a red haired dachshund named Graham Cracker, cries at the front window every time the ice cream man's truck drives by. She loves ice cream and hearing Nicholas tell of the lengthy conversation his Mom had with Graham Cracker about how ice cream is not good for dogs, sent us both into hysterics. To be clear, we were not making fun of the dog, but rather the funny image of his Mom eye to eye with Graham Cracker having a serious discussion. When the waitress came to take our order, we were both in the midst of a serious giggle fit. So I am fairly certain that we too were being observed during our moment of hysteria.

Recalling that last visit here with Nicholas makes me smile, as I draw my attention back to the people surrounding me today and it makes me think about the lives behind these faces.

Is there someone with a broken heart? Is someone ill or about to know they have some lifelong disorder? Who is lonely? Who is dealing with addiction? Who is depressed? What tragedies have happened to some? And which people sit here not knowing of the tragedies about to happen?

And likewise...what joys are unexpressed during this snapshot moment? When did that boy sitting to my left first experience eating ice cream? When did that young woman to my right first fall in love? Who is that man's best friend? Who has just gotten a new job? Who is expecting a baby and doesn't know it? Who has felt peace? Who has gotten an answer to a prayer? Who will explore a dream...tomorrow...the next day...or ten years from now?

There are so many untold stories here every day.

Same diner...same menus...same ticking of a clock...measuring time in moments...as the dreams and tragedies behind the faces...trickle in with the crowds...in a never ending stream.

SOLILOQUY

Tender expressions

A soliloquy unspoken

Reflects joy in a pair of eyes

Moments treasured

As the bonding of two transpires

A smile imprinted forever

On the others' heart

GOODBYE

His hands are worn out carpet

The threads barely holding together

He packs boxes

Throwing things in

Carefully placing others

Barren bedroom

She stands alone

Quivering lips ask how she'll cope

Focusing on her feet he says, "Goodbye"

DEAR ...

Dear Ex: I'll always care about you and I remember the good times because there were a lot of those and I hope you remember that too.

Dear Self: Keep pushing forward and keep writing.

Dear Mom and Dad: I miss you every minute of every day.

Dear Crush: You inspire my creativity effortlessly and I love that.

Dear School: I am thankful for everything I have learned (except for St. Joseph's School. I am not thankful for grades 1-3 with you! Ugh!)

Dear Sibling: I will always have your back and you will always have my love.

Dear Past Me: Put yourself first for a change and take much better care of yourself.

Dear Future Me: Be fearless and live in the moment.

Dear Future Child: I would be so honored to be your dad.

Dear Person I Love: You can call me 24-7 whenever you need me.

Dear Best Friend: You are my artistic other half and I love you more than I can verbalize.

Dear Ex-Best Friend: I no longer miss our friendship. It's been so many years but I wish you the best and hope you are happy.

Dear Haters: Thank you for the attention.

Dear People Who Love Me: Thank you.

IMPATIENT ENERGY

My pen is distracted tonight

By the events of the week

Lately, I despise the stress the days bring

Thank goodness for music and my headphones

I depend on them

To take me back to my center

Outside I hear the sound of distant fireworks

The high school football team must have won again

My eyes scan the window for inspiration

Resting my chin in my hand

A long sigh

And then … nothing

Fingers numb

The castle of crumpled papers below

Are abruptly collapsed by the notorious, whistling wind

<sigh>

This impatient energy

Has been trailing me since morning

Just like the unbroken chain of dewdrops

Drizzling onto my open windowsill

Sleep is still far away

But mystical thoughts suddenly fill my mind

Pampered, dreamy thoughts

Lift my desires back on the palette

LOVE

Love

It's often unexpected

These chance encounters

These connected conversations

It's alive in these moments

These fleeting glances

These singular flashes of clarity

It's in the pauses

These intermittent dreams of now

These moving drops of being

It's in these touches

These delicate wisps of home

These mendings of the mind

It's in these fragile seconds

These blinking eyes

These pulsing veins

THE SCENT OF RAIN

Though miles away

I can feel you near

I breathe you in

Like the scent of rain

AMID THE STILLNESS

He sits alone

Amid the stillness

Back up against the door

Painting the silence in words

On his canvas of clarity

UNDONE

He's come undone

The days go by

And the years have too

His life is a mirror

The reflection staring back is

Something he can no longer bear to see

His inner voice is so far away

Because the present

Is just something to get through

Leaning up against

Gapstow Bridge in Central Park

He stands in the cold

With the sun in his hair

Looking at the water below

He is a million miles away

Off in the distance

He hears the familiar sound

Of carnival music

Playing in time with his growing heartbeat

He ventures off

Towards the music

And finds himself

Standing at the carousel

Where he daydreams of his past

As a young boy

Riding on that same white horse

2370

At the Silver Lake summer carnival

In a rare moment of spontaneity

He hails a taxi

And directs the driver to take him to Silver Lake

Where he has not been in thirty years

He bids the city farewell with a smile

Choosing to enjoy this long, expensive ride back to a time and place

When his heart was still wild

His mood floods with nostalgia

As the car pulls up to the edge of Silver Lake

And after instructing the driver to wait

He takes the long walk to the end of the boardwalk

To the gazebo

Where as a boy

He carried with him his beloved music box

Holding it carefully on his lap

He would stare for hours at the families of turtles

Swimming gingerly atop the silvery lake

While the music played on and on

Until one day

In a fit of rage

After being teased by the other kids

For carrying around a "little boy's toy"

He tossed the music box into the lake

And watched it slowly disappear

Until it was no longer visible under the water

He was 14 years old

Now

He sits on the wooden boards of that same gazebo

Dangling his legs over the edge

And astoundingly

Inside his head

He hears the music that he has not heard in thirty years

The music of his cherished music box

He closes his eyes softly

Until he becomes part of the music

He sits there for over an hour

Until he is able to evoke

The joy

Inside

His reawakened wild heart

FATHER AND SON

Miles of stars are between us

Yet I feel your every heartbreak

Every joy

They are the same stars

That mirrored in your young eyes

Sparking our bond

Tonight there are no stars in view

But that doesn't matter much

Because our father/son connection is stronger

Than the dark, scary clouds

That adorn this ominous sky

FOR JORGE AND HIS DAD

The memory of us

Stays with me

Intricately woven

Into all that I am

Into all that I ever hope to be

And it will linger on forever

For in the lingering

Is where I can find you

And nobody can take you away

Because we are forever connected

SUMMER NIGHT

Wriggling my toes I watch the sand trickle out like those in an hourglass. The goosebumps on my arms stand like mountain peaks as I dig my feet deeper into the fading warmth of the beach. The blue water now is pitch black and the laughing inside has changed to shouting. I dare not go up those porch stairs. Instead I choose to stay here and wait patiently for the arguing to end. I sit in silence not moving lest I alert them to my presence. I cradle the long spire between my hands. The pink deep inside echoing the evening surf and the edge ruffles like the skirt of a ballerina. Putting it to my ear, I let the sea drown out the screaming. I suppose I could go in and try to get between them, but that would just make things worse. I decide instead to sit this one out.

The last time I intervened, Justin's girlfriend, Megan, referred to me as a bad influence as I fired venomous words right back. It was not pretty. And the next day there was a silence you could cut like a knife. She knows I see right through her charade which is why she despises me so. After my altercation with Megan, I felt terrible for days because I upset Justin and I promised myself I would never do that again. Justin will see her for her true colors eventually. It's just so impossibly difficult to watch your friend fall in love with someone so full of deceit and toxicity.

243

Mr. Snyder steps out on to his deck next door. I know he can hear the commotion so I try to reassure him that everything is okay by smiling and waving as he looks over. The steaks he throws on the grill sizzle. He smiles and waves back. I watch the whole family lounging out smiling and laughing settling around the picnic table. Closing my eyes I can almost imagine being there. The clinking of silverware on the plates and murmuring broken by the occasional squeal then finally the scraping of wood on wood and the clattering of plates being stacked.

At last I open my eyes. The sky now dark and the evening quiet at last. I stand up and dust the clinging sand from me. Treading softly, I climb the steps.

THE ONE

Tiptoeing through the filmy tendrils of my mind

Comes the one I seek

Only to disappear

Off on a gust of wind

Leaving me behind

In the darkness that mends ...

CRAYONS IN A BOX

Multicolored

Multifunctional

One without the other

They are nothing

A pack with just one color

Worthless

They complete each other

Not one color is left out

They are all equal

These crayons in this box

Just like you and me

Different colors ...same value

AFTERMATH

With every thought of you

The sky is enriched

My eyes widen

My heart opens

And feels

***Thank you, Jerome, my forever friend. RIP

BROKEN DREAM

The sporadic rain conducts

This afternoon's shadow dance

With the sun

I follow the cracks on the sidewalk

As they weave in and out

Of the sun and rain

Determined to stalk their every path

They branch out in all directions

Looking just like a flowchart

To an intricate, but broken dream

WE FOUND LOVE

One night

Not long ago

We sat together

Under the glow

Of an old time cinema

All ups

No downs

It spun me around

And back to your shining emerald eyes

Where love is found

YOUR WEDDING

You were standing there

Encircled by white wedding lights

On the arm of someone else

And I was standing there

With a bruised heart

When our eyes collide

A trace of us appears

And maybe a part of you knows

That he won't love you

Like I love you

Because he doesn't know you

The way I know you

As I make my way up

To the receiving line

You smile

Thinking my nervousness is cute

But you also have an intense look in your eye

I try to speak

But my words tumble imprecisely

All around your feet

I freeze

Glaring back in disbelief

At the vicious realization

That someone has taken you away from me

WORDS AND KALEIDOSCOPES

Words are like kaleidoscopes

Pointing up at the light

Their many hues

Twirl and spin around our heads

They scatter our thoughts

As they beckon

Before permanently taking shape

To christen our blank empty pages

NOBODY HOME

I ran for shelter

To the one place

Where I knew comfort lived

But even there I was

Shut out

Left all alone

Tired of the disappointment

And wet and withered from the rain

I turn up the music

And release it all

In between songs

I hear that

Tomorrow there is a chance

For sunlight

And I know by then

You will be gone from my

Thoughts

My life

My future

<u>DYING</u>

As time marches on

Beneath weathered skin

A heart fills and flows

Winded with age

So many voiceless dreams penned

Now unwind towards an end

Fades and whispers

Of songs unsung

Linger in the air

And they are the last sounds heard

Before the heart

Wearily slows down

To

Rest

BEFORE AND AFTER

Long before we met

And shared a mingling of desires

Your image was a presence I knew

That lived behind my eyes

Like a memory

From somewhere in history

Long before I heard you whisper

My name was in your breath

In a quiet knowing tone

Spoken by you and you alone

PERFECT TOGETHER

Talk to me about something only we know

Like when we used to escape

On the golden days of fall

Following the painted leaves as we hiked

We preferred

The hard to reach destinations

Because they were empty and quiet

Belonging only to us

It always felt so perfect

When we would lay in the stillness

And silently dream in unison

Sometimes I miss your raspy whisper

Stalking my ears

Back when everything you said

Was sacred to me

GRIEF

Tears on the pillow

He cries alone …

<u>LANDSLIDE</u>

I hear your whisper everywhere

Teasing me with embryonic sound

The sunlight that beams brightly

Is the same sun that reflected in your eyes

And lit our love

Gazing up at this sunlit November sky

The sad and lonely vision I woke with

Dissolves

Once the music is cued

I close my eyes softly

And while Stevie sings about growing older

I see us curled up on my sofa

We feel the music

It evaporates our loneliness

Allowing everything in our minds to

Melt into one another

Even after all these years

I hope you still feel this

And remember us this way

Whenever "Landslide" plays

YOUNG AND STILL INNOCENT

He stands at the window

Of the empty dorm room

Watching his godson and his friends

Playfully "performing "and being silly out on the quad

Thinking how it is good

That some of the wicked truths of life

Are kept from the young

THINGS I LOVE ABOUT YOU

I love that you look me in the eye

I like when you smile

And the way you run your hands over your face and through your hair when you're a little stressed

I love you in purple

I like that your LA Dodgers baseball hat is still on the front seat of my car

I love how vulnerable you can be

I like how much you love your mom

It's kind of cute when you get upset about losing to me at Scrabble

I love that you ate all of the candy canes off of my Christmas tree

I like watching you browse through my bookcases and how smart you are

I guess I pretty much like everything about you …

UNTANGLED HEART

All alone

With his heart tangled in knots

His thoughts

Turn to you

And the knots come undone

WALKING ON

For Danni

We walk on

Through the joy

Through the pain

Sometimes alone

And sometimes with others

 But this journey

This life

Of good and bad moments

Belongs

Only

To

Us

FOOTPRINTS

Walking along the shore

Waves crash around my ankles

I search for the perfect seashell

A keepsake for this place and time

I exist on a different plane

Between the sand and sea

It is here I can forget

And pretend that I don't care

My footprints in the sand

The tide washes them away

A faded hard memory

Like I was never here

SLEEPY SKY

Tonight

The pitch black sky

Is a reminder

That even the sun must sleep

ONCE AGAIN THE TIMING IS OFF

As we stand here in my kitchen

For a few moments

Smiling at each other

I realize

That for the first time in nearly a year

I am genuinely happy

Behind your striking smile

I see a mixture of pride and sadness

Proud because you have just landed your dream job

Sad because it is 3,000 miles away

In my head

I am thinking

Would you stay if I asked?

Which makes me feel ashamed

For being so incredibly selfish

As I turn my eyes away

A near silent sigh escapes me

Prompting you to sidle up next to me

"Are you okay?" you ask

"I am, actually" I say and lean my head on your shoulder

You rest your head on mine

And it's okay

For this brief fleeting moment in time

Everything is perfect

We can worry about the future

And those looming 3,000 miles tomorrow

MY EYES MISS YOURS

There are traces of you

All over my phone

And they make me miss you even more

I pull out my journal

And begin to write

About the way you looked at me on the day we said goodbye

You must have noticed

How much my eyes need to see you

In order to continue to shine

RESTLESS

The sound of rain on a tin roof

Used to hum me to sleep

Drowning out the voices

Of anger and doubt

The moonlight that

Shines in my window

Urges me to look up at the stars

I watch the curtains

Dance in the breeze

Like ghostly apparitions come

To befriend me in the night

And they whisper to me

Telling me to hold tight

To the moonlight and never let it go

I always dream in vibrant color

And many times

I dream I am flying

Soaring, free at last!

Still, when I hear the rain

Pitter-pattering on the roof

I hug my pillow tight

And face the window

Knowing the light of day

Will eventually come

THE OCEAN AT NIGHT

I do believe I am more of a night person than a day person. I love evenings best. It is the best time for dreamers to get lost in their velvety rich thoughts. The night sky beckons you to come outside and settle in amongst the stars and sit on a grassy knoll and hear the crickets. Or swing on the porch swing until your eyes grow droopy and the baseball playing on the radio seems like a lullaby.

I am thinking about this tonight in the midst of this stormy September night.

Have you ever been to the ocean at night?

Oh it is glorious. It is quite a different place in the evening than it is during the bright hours of daylight. The crowds have long gone home to dinner or to sleep and it is now a quiet place except for the roar of the ocean. Under the cloak of night, the heat has dissipated into whispers of cool breeze. You hug yourself to keep the chill away as you walk along the line of the shore. You feel the intimacy of the ocean so near. If you were daring enough you would sink into the now cool waters and feel the salty spray tingle melt into your calves. The waves tease you with their endless invitations to feel their nightly fury. The hypnotic beating heart of the sea is compelling and inspires thought and contemplation. The moon illuminates your hands and turns them white like

273

moonflowers. Goosebumps rise up on the back of your arms as you feel the ocean breeze turn colder. You stand there silently still, under the blue moon and you think to yourself that this feeling....this clarity and sense of peace you have…extinguishes the uneasiness you felt before. You secretly hope that this tranquility you feel will linger, and, as you turn to leave for home, you notice that the moon follows your every step.

KNOTS I'VE YET TO UNTIE

The knots are too hard to untie

Now that you have drawn the curtains on us

It is a sad notion to think

That you'll never know my secrets

Or about how much I believe

I had finally found something parallel

My eyes blink at lightning speed

Keeping the pounding raindrops out of my line of vision

So I can relish one last glance at you

Before saying goodbye for good

IN SPITE OF THE DARK

Technicolors brighten

Illuminated by unseen forces

Smiling through the darkest shadows

Aglow

THE ELUSIVE MISSING PIECE

Lying here

Listening to the pounding chorus of these two hearts

Leads me to believe

That maybe they have found

Their elusive missing piece

VALENTINE'S DAY-2018

Chocolate

Tastes

Like

Loneliness …

NO LONGER LOST

Subtle

Like the drifting clouds

You slipped into my senses

Quietly

Just like whispers in the wind

Quickly

You exposed my wall of defenses

From you

I expected nothing

Easily … I gave in to your passionate notions

You covered me in this radiant light

And patiently

You helped me see

279

That I was no longer lost

Stumbling in the dark

SURREAL

Back to back

Face to face

Cheek to cheek

Light to light

The tips of passion

Touch as fingertips

It's so surreal here

Like we are both jumping out from

A brilliant watercolor painting

Two intimate souls dancing in the dark

What odd bedfellows we are

When gentle turns to night

And the savagery simmers

Broiling our blood

Burning our flesh

We ride upon waves

Of molten liquid that rises to the top

Only to fall

When we can't quite feel the brush of human contact

Instead the words come

Page by page ...

<u>SORRY ...</u>

We kiss

I remember

Someone else

<u>TREASURE CHEST</u>

Our hearts belong

To the night

We are one in vision

One in a dream

Inside this

Unopened

Treasure chest

Of

Magic

THE DAY I MET KAI

Remember when I met you at the library?

The passionate burst of words

That fell from your lips

When you talked about writing music

And your desire to be very famous

Showed me that you possessed the heart of an artist

You read between my lines

With notable ease

When I gave to you

My books of my poetry

I remember how you smiled at me

Saying we should be friends

And how we spoke for hours

On that Saturday in January

I'll never forget

When the library was closing

And we stepped outside

Onto the frozen ground

You were looking up

As the sky was looking down

You said that you envied the bright stars

I looked and you and said, "I think you are going to be
brighter than they all are…"

THE POWER OF A LOOK

There is a moment

When a single look

Can express more love

Than all the poetry

Ever written

TAKE IT AWAY

Kiss

The

Loneliness

Out

Of

Me

INSIDE A MEMORY

Sometimes I hide inside the memory

Of you dancing with me

While I sang to you that old Fleetwood Mac song

We loved playing on the jukebox at Dudley's

Tonight

As this cover band takes the stage

And the drummer counts four

My heart beats in harmony

Your life is like its melody

Because just like you

It always seems to touch

The outside edge of my heart

TWO MELTING HEARTS

The world feels like music

When I lie next to you holding hands

Bright skies light up the room

Warm summer winds twirl and spin

Eyes gaze openly back

Keeping time with our melting hearts

MICHAEL'S GRADUATION

When I sat down to write this, I had no idea where to begin. There were so many things I felt should be said. So, I did what I always do when confronted with writer's block: I turned to music for inspiration.

I found myself outside on my front porch watching the sun set through the trees. It was so beautiful that I stopped and watched it for a while, marveling at how all the different colors could blend so perfectly together to form something that magnificent.

Seeing this makes me think of you, Michael, and the journey you have had to get to this point, here, at your high school graduation. There are so many factors that went into building the young man you are, and there are so many beautiful things that make you who you are. There is something so grandiose waiting for you at Cornell. Your whole life is ahead of you, and there's beauty in just that fact.

I enjoy using the analogy of the sunset, in part, because the future, then, for you, is the nighttime. For me, the night signifies a new beginning. And as Bruce Springsteen says, there is magic in the night, and I do believe that because there is always some light guiding you through the darkness, whether you realize it or not. The moon, obviously, is the one most people think of, and it's what keeps most people on course, but when the moon isn't there then there are so many other little guiding lights to keep you on the right path, like fireflies. A night cannot be complete without fireflies. What lies ahead for you, no one knows, but those fireflies will always be there, no matter what, to light the way through the darkness. I wish you a multitude of fireflies in life.

There will be hardships down the road. I would be doing you a disservice if I were to try to deny that. There are so many responsibilities awaiting you that hardships are inevitable. The only advice I can offer is to learn to welcome them. It's just another color to add to the beauty of the sunset. And sunsets continue forever, you can count on them just as you can count on me being on your side forever.

THE PASSING OF YEARS

After all of these years

I still hold your hand

Though these

Childhood days

Have passed

FEAR-LOVE-WALLS

This heavy heart

Is a mixture of emotions

A whirlwind of sensations

Past hurts create walls of fear

Love comes knocking

Seeking entrance

The heart is eager

But …

Fears prevail

Eyes intense with longing

Walls are crumbling

The heart is still heavy

<u>ALIVE</u>

Inspired by Michael Galante

On rain filled days

You can lose sight of the sun and the moon

But you know they are there

They always come back from behind those clouds

And the dreams that lie inside our heads

Are what make us feel alive

DECEMBER WIND

There are some

Words

That even the December wind

Cannot

Unweave

WHY CAN'T YOU LOVE ME?

The stained glass table

Where we sat that morning

Reflected brightly in the light of dawn

But our mood was anything but sunny

We ate our breakfast in silence

Until I asked," Why can't you love me?"

The words settled on the table

Like little crumbs of something toxic

You set your jaw

Clenching your teeth so hard

I was afraid they would crumble

A weighty silence commenced

Your words never came

But when you looked down

Avoiding my eyes

I had my answer …

FIRST TRIP OF THE SEASON

When I step onto the shore

For the first time this season

I take a deep breath

And inhale the salty taste of the sea

My fingers dance

As they glide across the sand

My mind races with each wave

When it makes it back home

I look up at the horizon

And see only infinite love

When I watch the sun set

In its orange-red fire glow ...

THE DANCE

Sun drops in

Softly at first

Beam after beam

Dancing atop the thirsty blue green water …

PAIN ON A PEDESTAL

I carry the world

On invisible shoulders

Tightly wrapped boxes

Of life's many stresses

Burden my weight

As if lifting heavy boulders

I smile to the world

But sometimes my eyes

Deceive even me

Interrupted sleep at 1am

I am up again writing

Unspoken feelings echo from deep inside

My pain on a pedestal

For the world to see

FOR JEROME

We share the same blanket of azure blue sky

You sound so close

Though there are millions of miles between

Our two souls

These distances of space and time ...

How strong they are

And how weak they are

Because I can feel you so easily

And sense your every movement

On the other end of the sky

Night arrives and renders itself to this dream

The moon beams brightly ...

As I trace your face in the stars

For the whole world to see

GET OUT OF MY HEAD!

Why are you here tonight … lingering …and eating at my thoughts?

Preying on my sleep?

I have no walls

Only a door

    For you to finally

       Close

MAKING MY ENTRANCE

The trees whisper my name

Making it resonate between the lampposts

Thunder rumbles low in the background

Waiting for the sky to light my stage

Clouds darken

Only to heighten my glory

The willow tosses her head

In utter defiance before me

I make my entrance on the wings of the wind

I am rain …

    Reciting my soliloquy

WELCOME BACK, INSOMNIA

Tonight

My mind has invited insomnia

Back in

Out the window

Beyond these rain drenched streets

I can hear the 2:30 am train

Clicking and clacking

Its way into the station

Whenever I ride the train

I collect glances from strangers

Moments stolen

From what might have been

Are recorded in my journal

Where they are stored

Forever

Nights like these

Are perfect

For revisiting

Such moments …

GHOSTED

After you "ghosted" me

My senses grew numb

Cold and thick

Impossible to be warmed

My mind lost control

Passing through the emptiness

Entering into darkness

Where the faint glimpse of love

 Shattered into a million pieces

Never to be whole again

Now I stand here all alone

Lost in between this void

And where love, dreams, and passion call

PUZZLE

Do you ever feel like a puzzle?

Always trying to piece together the complete picture

Of who we are

Sometimes we get it wrong

And sometimes we are left unfinished

Perhaps this is for the best

Because pieces can't be forced into a puzzle

Or at least they shouldn't be

That wouldn't make sense

RUSH

I found that spot

On your bottom lip

And I nibbled

Enjoying your reaction

Drawing you closer

So close our eyelashes

Tap together

 As Sarah sings …

"Nothing stands between us here"

We are

Intermingled

Open

Giving

Taking

Ah…such wonderful intimacy!

And a warm rush

That is

Completely unforgettable

DO I GIVE LOVE ANOTHER CHANCE?

The storm rages

Lightning strikes

The thunder bellows

Deeply

Moving in time

To the beating rhythm

Of this anxious heart

In my head

I ponder the toughest question

Do I give love another chance?

And fight through the pain I feel inside

After being "ghosted?"

I wipe the damp mud of uncertainty

From my shoes

And continue to walk in the pounding rain

In search of these answers

A WRITER'S LIFE

Red lines

All across the writing tablet

Delete this phrase

Or thought

Crumpled brow

Retraces foggy slopes

Searching …

Connecting the past

To the present

With common threads

Pained eyes stare

In blankness

At a poem

Waiting its turn …

<u>HIDING OUT TOGETHER</u>

Come sit with me

On this exiting summer night

We'll hide out on the back porch

And count the invisible stars in a milky sky

Until our eyes

       Grow

              Heavy

                     And

                           Tired

DIFFERENT BEACH-SAME OCEAN

Intermittent shadows

Fall in front of us

Up above, the South Carolina sky is hot and hazy

Below, toes squish in the sand

Down at the water's edge

Waves dance and tickle our feet

Sea breeze whips past our heads

Sandcastle for two

Decorated with shell and stone

Washes out to sea

We too depart

With the arrival of high tide

Now, more than 20 years later

A different beach, but the same ocean

I bring my thoughts down to the water's edge

The intimacy of the ocean fills in for you

Thundering silence is broken when

A solitary gull cries out from above

These days I walk the shoreline all alone

God ... I feel so small ...

BOUNDLESS LOVE

Love knows no boundary

Reaching beyond common ground

With a simple touch

Empty hearts

Can be renewed

A DAUGHTER'S LOSS

For Kathryn

She sits with her back to the wall

Cuddling a smiling picture of her dad

And abandoned cup of Yorkshire tea sits beside her

Still steaming and oddly inviting

Her eyes stare off into a safe place

Remembering the exciting life her father led

The silence of the room

No longer screams obscenities

As lances of sunlight announce

The arrival of another day

FOR b.c.

Each of us craves a happy ending in this life

But for some

This is the beginning

Of a long, hard, battle

So reach back and pull someone else up

Put them in a straight line

Show them kindness and understanding

Too many lives and loves

Fall through the cracks

So it's time to get back to the music, the poetry, and the arts

And sing, write, and paint about sunrises and bright eyes

As my friend, Mary, says …

"Get some sunshine in your favorite chair."

And take in all that life has to offer!

EMPTY BEACHES

Sunset rays smile upon

The glassy surface

Of the still ocean water

Sparkling like precious gems

While pillow shaped clouds

Move across the sky

<u>NOVEMBER STREET</u>

Sometimes it's hard to watch

The way my bedroom window

Plays with the wind through the leaves on the trees

Today it reminds me

Everything leaves this world

So I turn up the music

"November Rain" is playing

I close my eyes

And let Axl's melody take me to another place

Pretending that life begins in the chorus

Of a favorite song

The pages of my journal

Document everything

From how you can prove the sun wrong

When it points out your faults

To how the autumn air tastes

Right after a kiss

For me, hope is all that is left standing

On this November street

PIRATE DAYS

The room is filled

With old books

And picture frames

Candles half burnt

And Mason jars

Overflowing with sea glass and foreign coins

Inside the mood is thick with a past

That resides under spider webs

And in treasure trunks

Bursting with relics

From a life spent chasing the extreme

Together with the one he loved most

Nowadays

Time just lingers

He sits beside the echoes

Staring off alone into the night

With the eyes of one who still craves adventure

Finding solace deep inside his imagination

CRYING RED

Sleepless nights

In an empty bed

A wounded heart

Crying red

YOU SAW ...

You felt my heart

Not my loathing

You saw my desires

Not my fear

And as the day surrendered to twilight

Your heart became mine

TOUCH

Our unbreakable bond

Is tied to my heart

My body reacts

When I see your name

Appear on my phone

And as your message plays

I picture your words

As they roll off your tongue

When I close my eyes

I can feel your arms around me

Brushing my back softly with your fingertips

I am half asleep

And loving every second

AWAKE

When I open my eyes

The morning light is blinding

But your smile brought me here

And pulled me through forever

WHY DOES SUMMER HAVE TO END?

Colors spill onto my pages

A kaleidoscope forms

In between

The sunbeams shining down

The suddenly placid wind

Plays with the dandelion wish flowers

At my feet

While the clouds patch the sky together

Creating blue and white words

That make me wonder

Why summer has to end

DO YOU REMEMBER?

When the day is ending

And the last trolley to pass his apartment is gone

Will you recall the sound of his voice and hear it echo
somewhere in the distance?

Or will it be one of his poems that nestles inside your head?

I wonder if you even recognize your own presence between
his lines ...

Will you remember his warmth and will you attach yourself to
memories of him on some cold, lonely night?

Or is this just too overwhelming for you to even imagine?

MISSING DEREK (1969-1997)

Thousands of days gone

Your absence still lies

Thick in my throat

Like an open wound

Waiting to heal

But when this dark room

Blankets my eyes

I feel you here

And I know

I will see you tonight

As my eyes

Finally close

FINAL ACT

I hear your music

And your soul touches me

Poetic lyrics with passionate eyes

Reach the landscape of my desires

The music takes me to my memories

Where I live for a moment

Still tendered by love

Showered with affections

Caressed by words

Dawn approaches

And I go to the window

Your music provides the soundtrack

As I watch the autumn leaves dance to the ground

Imitating us

In our final act.....

FOREVER FRIENDS

We are two parts

Tossed into oblivion

In each we have found a friendship

A missing piece

Two dreamers

In separate lives

Living out separate moments

We are enchanted by inner life

And eagerly seek

To uncover the magic

That few can see …

TO THE YOUNG ARTISTS

Inspired by Jerome Gonzalez

Enhance this world

With the hidden thoughts and ideas

That occupy your mind

And be brave enough

To spill your words on paper

For all to see

Unravel the kaleidoscopic colors

And create wondrous designs

Leaving nothing bare

Paint every inch

And let no one stop you

Because this world is your canvas

POSTSCRIPT

It's a funny thing when you let someone into your little world that you have created for yourself and then you suddenly realize you are incapable of imagining it without them …

Thank you to my readers. Without you, my words would have never left the confines of my journals, and for that I am eternally grateful.

Robert A. Cozzi

Afterword

As you have just finished a reading of Robert's best poetry yet in Kaleidoscope of Colors, I have just begun my thoughts. When I was first asked to take this on, I was somewhat worried, I will admit. His talents in writing are met only by the accomplishments that he has enjoyed. But I digress, as I would like to shed some light on my honest opinion of this latest collection of poetry, and what amounts to be his most well-written, and his best.

During the making of this collection, just a few days before I had the fortune of reading the manuscript, Robert consulted with me on the matter of sequencing his book. Which, if you've read his previous collections, you'll know that would be a new facet to his work. I read the manuscript and I pondered the idea for a few hours. And I came to the conclusion no sequencing was needed.

That is due to the relation between the title of this work and the material it encompasses. Kaleidoscopes are much like we are, or more specifically, our emotions. They are full of different shapes, colors, brightnesses. Our perception of emotions are similar. Some, like love, are associated with red or pink, and anger, passion, are associated with red. Sadness is typically conveyed through blue. Our emotions are varied, and shouldn't simply be categorized. Kaleidoscopes are ever-changing, much like us.

After reading this collection, I thought it would be most beneficial and most fitting that the book not be sequenced, and while it would be very well done, and deep, and honest, and powerful like all of Robert's work, it would not be the same if it were sequenced. By not sequencing it, he allowed each poem to hold its own weight, and reside in its own special spot, rather than serving a title. The poems in their variety correlate with the title, and that is a display of the thoughtfulness that Robert put into this wonderful, compelling work of art.

-b.c. Hudalla, writer and poet